LEARNING WITH LULU

Elisa 'Celeste' Cavazos Mullen

AuthorHouse™
1663 Liberty Drive
Bloomington, IN 47403
www.authorhouse.com
Phone: 833-262-8899

Because of the dynamic nature of the Internet, any web addresses or links contained in this book may have changed
since publication and may no longer be valid. The views expressed in this work are solely those of the author and do not
necessarily reflect the views of the publisher, and the publisher hereby disclaims any responsibility for them.

Any people depicted in stock imagery provided by Getty Images are models,
and such images are being used for illustrative purposes only.
Certain stock imagery © Getty Images.

This book is printed on acid-free paper.

ISBN: 978-1-4918-3421-3 (sc)
ISBN: 978-1-4918-3422-0 (e)

Library of Congress Control Number: 2013920962

Print information available on the last page.

Published by AuthorHouse 10/30/2020

authorHOUSE®

About the Author

Elisa Celeste Cavazos Mullen lives in San Antonio, Texas with Patrick, her husband of thirty-five years. They have a son, Michael, who works in the entertainment industry in Los Angeles.

'Celeste' is a bilingual Speech-Language Pathologist and has worked as a Special Education and Early Childhood educator. In addition, she has taught both English and Spanish as a second language to adults. For the past several years, she has worked with children and young adults who are within the autism spectrum. Currently, she is working in an Early Childhood Intervention Program.

Dedication

to Michael A. Mullen

· · · · · · · · · · · · · · · · · ·

Acknowledgements

Patrick Mullen

Ruben Cortez

Rick Castillo

Lulu is a small dog. Lulu pays attention and follows the command.

"Sit, Lulu."

"Yes, good job!"

"Shake hands, Lulu."

"Good job!"

Yeah. (clap hands)

"Down, Lulu."

"Good job!"

"Give me a 'high five', Lulu."

"Thank you."

Lulu likes to play Peek-a-Boo.

"Come, Lulu."

"Good job!"

"What happened?"

Lulu likes to exercise. She goes for a walk.

A butterfly lands on her head. "Fly butterfly, fly away."

Lulu is dancing. Dancing is fun for Lulu.

Lulu likes to eat cereal with apple. Yummy!

She has a healthy heart. Lulu wants you to eat healthy.

Lulu ate all her food.

The bowl is empty.

All gone.

Lulu is all done.

All done.

Lulu plays with a sock, a cloth ring, a ball, and a rope.

Lulu is barking: "Arf, arf."

Lulu likes to play with toys made of cloth.

Lulu's favorite toy is the rope.

Lulu watches the robot move. Lulu likes the robot.

Lulu likes to ride in the red car.

Lulu likes to ride in the car with her brother, Wally.

"Go, car."

"Go, go."

"Go, car! Go!"

Wally and Lulu share the red car. Wally likes to ride in the car.

He is happy.

Lulu is ready to get out of the car. She says, "I want to get out."

"Help."

"Please, help."

"Help me."

Lulu likes her toothbrush. She likes clean teeth.

Lulu is sad.

She does not feel well.

Big Bear comforts her.

Big Bear tells Lulu, "You are going to be okay."

Lulu gives Big Bear a hug.

Lulu waves goodbye.

"Bye."

"See you later."

Lulu is ready for bed. She sleeps with her toy dog and little bears.

"Good night."

"Night, night."

"Sh, sh." Lulu is sleeping.

Lulu says, "I love you."

About Lulu

Lulu, a Maltese, is a 'rescued dog.'

She has adapted well to her new environment, where she routinely receives good care, love, and protection.

She responds to her routine schedule, positive stimulation and shows a desire to please. She is very social and enjoys attention, especially playing with children.

Naturally smart, Lulu was cooperative and patient in her role showing how learning is fun and nurturing.

Printed in the United States
By Bookmasters